Jim Bennet Rhymes Again

Jim Bennet Rhymes Again

Light Hearted Verse from the Laureate of Atlantic Humour

Formac Publishing Company Limited
1989

Illustrations by: Catherine MacLean

Canadian Cataloguing in Publication Data
Bennet, Jim, 1931 -
  Jim Bennet rhymes again
  ISBN 0-88780-076-9
I. Title.
PS8553.E56J55 1989   C811'.54   C89-098676-2
PR9199.3.B46J55 1989

Published with the assistance of the Nova Scotia
Department of Tourism and Culture

Formac Publishing Company Limited
5502 Atlantic Street
Halifax, Nova Scotia
B3H 1G6
Printed and bound in Canada.

Contents

Foreword

The witty wordsmith is a rare, endangered species in contemporary society, and the rhyming Canadian sub-genus still rarer. Among such *rara avae*, Jim Bennet is a specimen truly worthy of preservation. Here he sets down his unique observations on life in the Canadian Maritime Provinces, particularly in his native Nova Scotia. Some Bennet songs, such as *Black Rum and Blueberry Pie, Nova Scotia Diet* and *Thick o' Fog* are established regional classics—though many natives still have no idea who wrote them!

For readers already enamoured of the Maritimes and for those unfortunates who continue to suffer from under-exposure, this collection of rhymes, songs and unabashed doggerel is a small treasure house of rhythmic anecdotes about the people of the Maritimes, their vagaries and their vices. Though written primarily for sheer fun, Jim Bennet's verses also document important facts of the social anthropology of the region. Adding further zest to the chowder, the doughty troubadour tosses in poetic tributes to several unsung heroes, real or imagined, from the mysterious world beyond the Atlantic shores. For our entertainment, joy and enlightenment, Jim Bennet rhymes again—heavens be praised!

Richard B. Goldbloom

Acknowledgements

Of the many people who helped in the production of this book, there are two in particular I would like to thank. One is my wife Laura, whose judgement I value above anyone else's. The other is my friend Dick Goldbloom, physician, musician, writer and skipper of the *Papillon II*, who provided the foreword.

J.L.B.

To Christie, Vicky, Neale and Amy

Birdwatchers and Other Heroes

The Man from Gaspereau

The story (possibly apocryphal) behind these verses is part of Annapolis Valley folklore. I first heard it from my mother, Helene Sandford Bennet, who was born of the stout Planter stock which settled the Valley in the 1700s. Acadia University of Wolfville is today less dominated by piousness than it was in the time of the mealy-mouthed minister of the legend.

'Twas many years ago around the Minas Basin shore,
When Wolfville's quiet classrooms hummed with academic
  lore
And scholars of Acadia with sober Baptist ways
Found college life a pleasant round of slow, idyllic days,
That out upon the bosom of the ruddy, muddy tide,
A boating party ventured for a day's most pleasant ride:
Six students from the college, with adventure all aglow,
Had hired themselves a boatman from the vale of
  Gaspereau.

The trip began propitiously: the students passed an hour
Admiring banks where apple-blossoms seasonally flower.
They sipped their seemly lemonade and munched their
  sugar buns
And marvelled at how swift and strong the Minas eddy
  runs;
But all too soon their steersman cocks a practiced weather
  eye
At darkling clouds that gather in the vaulted valley sky,
And as the chill nor'easter down the channel starts to blow,
His heart begins to hanker for his hearth in Gaspereau.

The students laugh and frolic as the spray begins to fly,
All loath to leave their outing while their fun is running
  high;
They coax their gallant coxswain harder still his back to
  bend
And take them further for his fare before the trip should
  end.

But soon they fall to bailing as the rising waves encroach
The oscillating gunwales of their wobbling water-coach
And join the panting oarsman at the flailing sweeps to row
Toward the spires of Wolfville and the homes of Gaspereau.

Too late! The boat is filling with the carmine-tinted flood
While still too distant lie the banks of sticky Minas mud.
Their loud laments are heard ashore, but none can offer aid
Before the flimsy craft is buried 'neath the cruel cascade.
The hands that grasp and grope for rescue lose their failing
    grip.
The sextet and their ferryman beneath the waters slip.
Ah, many are the hearts this night shall ache with grievous
    woe
In dorms of pious Wolfville and in humble Gaspereau.

'Tis legend how, a few days thence, the funeral bell rang out
To summon folk from campus and from country round
    about.
They gathered in their hundreds for a laudatory word
Before all mortal relics of the seven were interred.
The minister, appropriately solemn, took his place
To recommend their spirits to the Lord's especial grace
And eulogized them thus, in tones both reverend and low:
"Six precious souls from Wolfville (and a man from
    Gaspereau)."

The scene that next ensued was at the Providential gate
And what took place, of course, is quite impossible to state.
But, like as not, in Paradise the hierarchy heard
The patronizing parson's every condescending word.
And maybe Peter called out from his office by the wall,
"You precious souls from Wolfville stand outside until I call.
If you can't wait, then go to Hell. I'm busy here, you know.
We're holding a reception for the man from Gaspereau."

Pitiful Kate

Even the most tragic of figures, if the truth were known, might hold to that sense of resignation expressed by the phrase, "Oh, well. It's a living." This civic-minded madwoman is one such.

Down by the shores of the sediment pond
At the Purification Facility grounds
Staggers a figure in tatters and ashes
Screaming a series of hideous sounds;
Eyeballs gyrating with pupils dilating,
Fluttering fingertips clawing the air,
Slavering, quavering, lurching and wavering,
Shivering, moaning and tearing her hair.
Head heaped with ashes, the derelict stumbles,
A woman whose story is sad to relate:
This the demented and lost individual
Known to the neighbours as Pitiful Kate.
Pinned to her dress is a yellowing photograph
Showing a face from the gone and beyond:
This is the lover, according to legend,
Who drowned long ago in the sediment pond.
Passers take pity on Kate in her anguish
Tossing odd coins on the path at her feet.
Fortune will favour the bountiful donor,
So goes the story that's heard on the street.
Thus, in as regular fashion as clockwork,
Nine to five daily and five days a week,
Pitiful Kate comes to walk by the silt-pond,
Comes to convulse, tremble, shiver and shriek.
Hear how she howls in the throes of her madness,
Hear the tormented cacophonous sound,
Loud lamentations and wild ululations
Rending the air in a riotous round.
Eventide comes to the Sewage Authority
Just as it comes to the village and fields,
And the night watchman, in passing her station,
Motions to Kate with the truncheon he wields.
Then, in mid-gibber, her wild invocations
She ceases, and straightens her whirligig eyes,
Walks down the road as the gate swings behind her

And hobbles toward home under darkening skies.
Home is a humble but orderly hut
At the edge of the Inter-municipal Dump.
Kate hangs her shawl on a hook by the doorway
And stands by the sink with the cast-iron pump,
Works at the handle till water comes flowing,
Washes the ashes from out of her hair,
Pours out some Beefeater, makes a martini,
Grills a small sirloin to medium rare.
After her supper she percolates coffee
And sits at a desk with a roll-away top,
Pulls on the chain of a purple and tangerine
Tiffany lamp from a smart little shop,
Takes a brown envelope, long and official,
Out of a pigeonhole, picks up a pen,
Opens the case of her silver-rimmed spectacles,
Dons and adjusts them most carefully, then
Reaches down folders of neat memoranda,
Notebooks and ledgers in tall, tidy stacks,
Spreads them before her in deep concentration:
Pitiful Kate is computing her tax.
Scanning the form from the Revenue Service
Open in front of her, waiting and blank,
Kate begins checking the year's calculations,
Multiple integers, rank upon rank.
Under her name, "Occupation" is called for
And, in the space on Page One, upper left,
Pitiful Kate with her fountain pen enters
"Self-employed madwoman, lover-bereft."
Later that evening, her counting completed,
She folds up the form in her calico lap,
Picks up the envelope long and official,
Puts in the paper and gums down the flap,
Neatly affixes a stamp in the corner,
Closes the desktop and picks up her shawl,
Opens the door and steps out where the moonbeams
Soft on municipal rubbish-heaps fall.
Slowly, she walks to the box by the roadside
Marked with the gold-painted Post Office crest
Where, after leaving the madwoman's fingers,
The document falls in a heap with the rest.
Then, duty done once again for a twelve-month,

Birdwatchers and Other Heroes / 5

Pitiful Kate turns her back on the box
Just as the first stroke of midnight is chiming
Both from the church and municipal clocks.
Pausing a moment to gather the ashes
Which on the morrow she'll mix with her hair,
Pitiful Kate makes her way home to slumber,
Conscience as clear as the crystalline air.

Howe Now

Joseph Howe, the Tribune of Nova Scotia, had everything: the pen of a firebrand, the stuff of a statesman, an eye for the ladies, a taste for travel around his home province, eloquence as a political campaigner, and the common touch. His successful two-day defense against libel charges brought a free press to Nova Scotia. His duel with a challenger in Point Pleasant Park proved his physical courage. And his statue on the grounds of the provincial legislature is still able to charm the birds out of the trees. You just can't seem to get help like that these days!

Howe, he loved his old port city.
Howe, he wrote with fearless pen.
Howe, his talk was warm and witty.
Howe, the folks adored him then.
Howe, he loosed his hearty lustings.
Howe, he won the deadly duel.
Howe, he rode the rural hustings.
Howe, he quaffed the fiery fuel.
Howe, he freed the daily scribblers.
Howe, he roamed his province o'er.
Howe, he scorned the petty quibblers.
Howe, he loved the voters' roar.
Howe, he fought Confederation.
Howe, he rode the rural track.
Howe, he fostered education.
Howe, we wish we had him back!

The Liars' Bench

There really was a Liars' Bench in Springhill, Nova Scotia, neatly labelled and located near the baseball diamond of the little coal-mining town, home of the then-famous Springhill Fence Busters. Both Bench and Busters have long since departed the Springhill scene, leaving us only the sport of speculation.

In old Springhill for years it stood,
A landmark of renown;
A humble thing of weathered wood
Yet apex of the town
Where cronies came to sit and rest,
Their thirst for talk to quench
And judge who told a tall tale best
Upon the Liars' Bench.
'Twas fringed with chips and shavings, mark
Of many a whittler's wrist
With stains around it, rich and dark,
From well-chewed Pictou Twist.
Opinion vehement and proud
In boldest terms was stated;
Each point was scored in accents loud,
Each claim exaggerated.
The talk might be of digging coal
In Cumberland's rich seam,
Of mortal man's immortal soul
Or wild Fence Busters team
Which on the diamonds of the East
Once played a mighty game
(Some one or two of whom at least
Had won a share of fame
Advancing to the foremost row
Of baseball's proud processional
And, moving up from semi-pro,
Had gone full-fledged professional.)
Of these and many another thing
The sages came and talked:
Of trout they'd caught some long-past spring,
Of deer they once had stalked,
Of escapades of lusty youth

With many a winsome wench,
All told with little thought for truth
Upon the Liars' Bench.
And now no more for public use
The Springhill scene it graces.
Of shavings and tobacco juice
You'll find no further traces.
Where stands it now? Nobody knows,
And yet it's in my nature
To wonder if it might repose
Within our legislature
Where, warmed by haunches sleek and plump
From Throne Speech to Recessional
Perhaps, at last, it's made the jump
And finally gone professional.

The Purdy Hurdy-Gurdy

The moral of this tale is "Never market your product, no matter how clever, without sufficient testing."

Of the brothers known as Purdy, one was terse and one
   was wordy.
Younger brother's name was Hardy, taciturn and often
   tardy;
Gordy was the older brother, garrulous, unlike the other.
One liked action; contemplation pleased his brother.
   Combination
Of their gifts was symbiotic, yielding concepts quite exotic
One of which (if one is ample to provide a fair example)
Was the famous hurdy-gurdy crafted by the brothers Purdy.
Ne'er seemed hurdy-gurdy finer: played in major keys and
   minor,
Chords augmented and diminished, and before the Purdys
   finished
It was programmed to deliver everything from Swanee
   River
As composed by Stephen Foster to a plainsong Pater Noster.
Andantino and scherzando, allegretto, rallentando
From its inner chambers churning as the crank was slowly
   turning
To impel the cogs and bellows fashioned by the Purdy
   fellows.
At a touch the box would go so smoothly into virtuoso
Renderings of Paganini, Haydn, Verdi and Rossini.
That machine played Grieg and Purcell perfectly, with no
   rehearsal.
Every Strauss from Rick to Oscar, opera from Boh/me to
   Tosca;
Music of all sorts it yielded as each knob and dial was
   wielded.
Once a patent was forthcoming, many thousands soon were
   humming
To the tuneful airs unwinding from the hurdy-gurdy's
   grinding.
Trouble, though, was in the offing: Rimsky started
   Korsakoffing,

Handel turned in wrong directions; what a Liszt of
   imperfections
From a tinny Pachelbel to a Bartok out of hell!
What once seemed the world's eighth wonder was revealed
   as quite a blunder.
Why the instrument turned sickly can be summed up rather
   quickly:
Seems the Purdy hurdy-gurdy wasn't hardy, strong nor
   sturdy.
Hindsight puts it in perspective: flashy, but design-defective.

The Party-Fleet, Scourge of the Seas

There are two reasons that cruising sailors drop anchor at night.
Some do it for quiet repose in lonely, unspoiled surroundings, where
they can be lulled to sleep by the ripple of tiny waves along the hull.
Others do it in packs for the purpose of partying until an hour before
dawn, to the tune of every amplified racket known to mankind.
Unfortunately, the two varieties sometimes choose the same cove.

The Grampus, Ringdove, Hopson's Nose, the Rackets and
   Mad Moll,
The Sisters, Dover Castle, Dollar Rock: I've passed 'em all
In ketch and schooner, yawl and sloop, Bermuda rig and
   .gaff,
In racing boat and cruising boat and in the half-and-half.
I've sailed in ground swells, chops and lops, in stormy seas
   and wild,
In weathers fierce and weathers bland, on halcyon days and
   mild.
I've cooked and conned and steered and swabbed and
   midnight watches kept.
I've slept while others hauled the sheets and hauled while
   others slept.
I've chilled my cheek in flying spume and burnt it in the
   sun.
I've lost my luncheon overboard and still could call it fun.
But when the long-sought moment comes, that calm and
   lovely time,
When hook is dropped in lonely cove for rest and peace
   sublime,
When sail is furled and mainsheet coiled and cabin lamp is
   lit,
When crew, once fed, may sit and read (or maybe merely
   sit)
Ah! that's the time that summons up the sailor's last reserve,
The trying time that tests the strength of courage, grit and
   nerve,
For that's the time when Neptune plays his grimmest little
   joke
As bliss is blasted hell-west and your smile goes up in
   smoke,

For just as silence close-enfolds each ocean-weary sailor
Someone steams in with searchlight on, and raises a
　　loud-hailer
To shatter the idyllic mood with amplified delight:
"There's room for all nine boats, you guys; the party's here
　　tonight!"

The Battle of Mingleberry Mews

Tennyson wrote of the Charge of the Light Brigade *in the far Crimea and Kipling of blood and bullets on Afghanistan's plains. This is the story of an engagement that took place within the usually peaceful confines of the City of Westminster, the point being that battle honours are where you find them.*

As Major Basil Bullister was toying with his tiffin
In the drawing room of Mingleberry Mews, 11-B,
About to munch a biscuit spread with Fortnum's Potted
    Bloater Paste
And take his deep initial draught of strong Darjeeling tea,
He set his Wedgewood teacup with a clatter on its saucer
And dropped his water biscuit on a presentation tray,
For in the street he heard a sound that galvanized his
    memory,
A sound he hadn't heard since back on Coronation Day!
The Major squared his shoulders as he peeked around the
    curtains;
His monocle confirmed the sound that made his hackles
    stand:
'Twas the drill-platoon and gun's crew of the Bangalore
    Light Borderers
Preceded by the colour-guard and regimental band.

The Bangalore Light Borderers were Bullister's old regiment,
A unit first recruited in the glory of the Raj
Among the weedy-tweedy chinless wonders and remittance
    men
Who flourished like the poppies in the shadow of the Taj.
And from beginnings quite as inauspicious as they might
    have been,
The Bangalores progressed in even less auspicious way
By going into battle in a skirmish west of Hindustan
When all their ammunition-mules were east of Mandalay
(Although, as luck would have it, nothing came of this odd
    circumstance
Because in fact the enemy was nowhere to be found:
Three days before they'd given up their ambuscade
    impatiently,

Presuming that the Bangalores had gotten turned around.)

And so it subsequently went in annals of the regiment
Although they tried of glory to amass a rightful share,
It always seemed their ranks were somehow out of step
   with destiny,
And when the Empire needed them, the Bangalores weren't
   there.
They'd wandered into Mafeking to find the siege was lifted
And they'd straggled into Lucknow as relief was being
   cheered.
They'd proudly reached Pretoria at signing of the Armistice
And left for the Sudan once General Gordon had been
   speared.
In short, they'd never filled the space allotted on their
   colours
For the list of battle honours: it was noticeably blank.
But their uniform was splendid from the fringes of their
   epaulets
To gold-encrusted frogging on insignia of rank.

And every great occasion of a nature ceremonial
Was sure to find the Bangalores resplendently on hand
With drill-platoon magnificent in tunics of incarnadine
Preceded by the colour-guard and regimental band.
The Major turned the key in his mahogany campaign-chest
And pulled his tunic out of it, gold epaulets and all,
Then donned his pukka helmet with the regimental ribbon
And the sword that hung beside it on the hat rack in the
   hall,
Came smartly to attention and saluted in the mirror,
Roared, "Present and accounted for," then smiled a jaunty
   smile
And formed close column of platoon, a difficult manoeuvre
For a single individual to execute in style.

The ornamental scrollwork on his scabbard was a-gleaming,
His eyes were shining brighter than a colour-sergeant's
   lance;
As Bullister came bursting through the Mingleberry
   archway

He hummed the proper bugle-call for, "Bangalores
  advance!"
Just then, around the corner came a Works Department lorry
With a load of four-foot sewer pipe for Mingleberry Road.
In passing over Bullister it somewhat overwhelmed him,
For the gravity of sewer-pipes is greater by the load.
He raised upon his elbow and collected all his faculties
(Remarkable, in view of just how thinly he'd been rolled)
And shouted to his comrades, "Steady! Steady on, the
  Borderers!"
In tones that, all considered, were both vigorous and bold.

The Officer Commanding heard the regimental rally-cry
And gave the order quickly for the Bangalores to halt.
Then, calling forth the gun's crew, shouted, "Three rounds
  load and quick-fire!"
Which order was obeyed without a serious default.
The louts upon the lorry shouted, "'Ere! Wot's this?" and
  countered
With a fusillade of sewer bricks and pieces of cement,
As with the sounds of battle of a terrible intensity
The air of quiet Mingleberry neighbourhood was rent.
For troops who'd been intent on duties purely ceremonial
(Rehearsing for a church parade, the date of which was
  past),
The Borderers responded with a splendid show of discipline
Although their sense of marksmanship was anything but
  vast.

Their camouflage abilities were instantly apparent,
Their skills in quick concealment were magnificently shown;
And if they didn't damage or discourage any sewer-men
Then neither did they injure more than seven of their own.
And when at last the bobbies 'twixt the Works men and the
  Borderers
Insinuated cordons of a temporary truce,
And when the local duty-squad despatched by St. John
  Ambulance
Decreed that further efforts on the Major were no use;
When Last Post had been sounded and a volley rattled
  raggedly,

The band had played the Dead March and the service had
    been read,
The Bangalores gave three cheers for the very first Light
    Borderer
In regimental history who hadn't died in bed.

And that is why mess dinners of the Bangalore Light
    Borderers
Today are punctuated, at the passing of the port,
By grave and solemn toasting to the veterans of combat
And anecdotal ramblings of a sentimental sort.
And that is why a monument by popular subscription
Was erected in the churchyard of St. Swithin-on-the-Lawn
With *To Our Fallen Comrade, Basil Bullister, the Hero*
Of the Bangalore Light Borderers well-chiselled thereupon.
And that is why the colours of that combat-hardened
    regiment
The space for battle honours may legitimately use,
And why, embroidered there beneath the lion and the
    unicorn,
Is one bold line of letters reading: Mingleberry Mews.

The Sculpin

The poor old sculpin—he's the one fish that even small boys with hook and twine disdain as a catch of the day. Someone, someday, may discover that he makes as delicate a meal as his more handsome cousins.

The sculpin's a fish that all fishermen wish
Would stay clear of hook, line and sinker;
For which high disdain the reason is plain:
The sculpin's a hideous stinker.
His head's oversize, he's got big, bulgy eyes
And his mouth is the shape of a scuttle.
Each fish in the sea is more handsome than he,
Including the lump and the cuttle.
Inelegant lines, all spindles and spines
With fins like a broken umbrella
And queer-looking gills decorated with quills
Make sculpin a strange-looking fella.
Why God ever made this marine-life charade
Is open to lively conjecture;
The sculpin was not His most adequate shot
At salt-water-fish-architecture.
But, though I confess I'm just taking a guess
Which may be, in fact, a bit steep,
Perhaps in His way He was trying to say
That beauty is only fin deep.

Citronella and the Hawk

*Surely there exists no more innocent occupation than birdwatching.
But to the serious practitioner it's a risky business as well. Boots full
of swamp water, stone-bruised shins and bramble scratches are just a
few of the hazards encountered by these doughty observers of Mother
Nature's airforce. Consequently, the hobby has its heroes; this is the
story of one of the bravest.*

There was an old bird-watcher known as Citronella Curd
Whose ultimate ambition was the watching of a bird
The field-manuals listed as "occasional at best"—
The Purple-Shinned Potato Hawk, a species known to nest
In old abandoned barley-mills, neglected castle keeps
And chimneys unattended to by masons or by sweeps.
She had a pair of gaiters made of stoutest service duck,
A shooting-stick the seat of which quite often came unstuck,
A pair of field binoculars with center-focus-wheel,
And for her ornithology an unremitting zeal.
And that is why we find her on November twenty-third
Just entering a barley-mill, convinced that she had heard
The loud, aggressive whistle terminating in a squawk
Attributed by bird-books to no other kind of hawk
Than that which bears the field-mark of shiny purple shins
And lives on baked potatoes torn by talons from their skins.
She uncased her binoculars on passing through the door
And focussed on the stairway to the ruined upper floor.
But, finding that the darkness of that long-decrepit mill
Was more than they could cope with, she resorted to her
  skill
In creeping forward silently on gaiter-bolstered legs
And dared to hope she might discern a parent hatching
  eggs,
Which feat would be the talk of bird-clubs greater than her
  own
And make her Spotter of the Year for all the Seventh Zone.
She even had a momentary dream of what she'd say
To start her dissertation, *The Potato Hawk Today*,
And how her colour photos of a handsome nesting pair
Would avidly be bargained for as rarest of the rare
By *Quill & Feather Magazine*, *The Spotter's Weekly* too,

And by the colour section of *The Monthly Bill & Coo.*
But as they do with mice and men, all plans may go awry
With weekend ornithologists whose dream may be to spy
Upon a *rara avis* in a habitat unsound,
For just as Citronella was nine steps above the ground
Preparing her binoculars, her camera and her pen
To annotate a moment that would never come again,
A rotten bit of timber in the staircase crumbled through
(As rotten bits of timber in abandoned buildings do)
Precipitating Citronella, birding-kit and all,
Into a musty corner of the barley-mill's back hall.
The buckle of her knapsack in the tumble came undone
And from it, consequently, rolled potatoes, one by one
That she had packed for lunch, along with ginger beer and
   cheese
(For of all picnic morsels she'd a preference for these).
Before those baked potatoes had entirely come to rest,
Miss Curd's elusive quarry left its second-storey nest
And with a squawking whistle and a flutter and a flap,
Swooped down upon that frightened soul and landed in
   her lap,
From which convenient perch it very quickly set about
Attacking the potato skins to get the middles out.
In barely thirty seconds time the hawkish work was done,
And where there once were three potatoes there remained
   not one.
Some ragged shreds of skin were all that marked the sorry
   scene
Of where, upon that tweedy lap, the hungry bird had been.
The hawk had flown, the lunch was gone, the
   spotting-glasses cracked,
The shooting-stick was broken and Miss Curd's left eye was
   blacked;
But, bravely persevering, she picked up the peelings there
And put them in the packsack with all tenderness and care.
Then home to write her journal dauntless Citronella went
Ere her recollection faded of the wonderful event.
The monthly meeting of the Seventh Zone was close at
   hand,
And soon before that body Citronella was to stand
Triumphantly displaying the most satisfied of grins
And one small bag of cellophane containing certain skins

Once part of three potatoes and the subject of a talk
Entitled *Bird of Purple Shins: The Rare Potato Hawk.*
Now of a winter evening Citronella loves to sit
And take out her potato-skins and reminisce a bit.
A rusty gate hinge in the wind evokes the whistling call,
The fireplace flickers feathered shadows on her parlour wall,
While very faintly outlined by the candle's cheery wick
A pair of broken glasses and a splintered shooting-stick
Are standing on a shelf by the bird books, row on row,
In silent confirmation of adventure long ago
On that momentous morning in the barley-mill's cool shade
When weekend-birding history by one brave soul was
    made.

Shane Potter

The likelihood of finding two socks from the same pair relates
inversely to the lateness and frustration of the seeker—an axiom
known as Potter's Rule of Stockings. It derives from a poor soul who
lost his reason to a drawerful of singles.

Shane Potter was a placid soul
Who lived austerely, in the main,
Contented with suburban role
And an existence calm and plain.
His daily round was free of pain
And seldom jarred by vexing shocks
With this exception: 'twas his bane
To have to look for matching socks.

Each day, when out of bed he'd roll
To start the day's routine again
With coffee-cup and brimming bowl
Of milk-and-sugared breakfast grain,
Before departing down the lane
And heading for the business blocks
By 7:10 commuter train
He'd first begin the hunt for socks.

He'd stand and scratch his frazzled poll,
He'd rack his sleep-befuddled brain
Then dance an anguished barcarolle
Before his bureau, but in vain.
His brow would knit, his face would drain,
He'd smite his thigh and shake his locks
Then bellow at his wife, "Elaine!
I can't find any matching socks!"

His temper, like an ember-coal
Was fanned, full fury to attain
Until he rampaged like a troll
Or frenzied pit-bear on a chain;
Just like mad Nero in mid-reign,
His scowls would stop the household clocks
As, "Damn and blast and hell!" cried Shane,
"I can't find any matching socks!"

In time such antics took their toll,
The fellow's health began to wane;
His stomach bore an ulcer-hole,
His nerves unravelled, skein by skein
Till he was carried, quite insane,
To padded cells with triple locks
Where, ever since, poor Potter's lain
In (matching) white asylum socks.

Lines for Patrick Flynn

In Mt. Olivet cemetery in Halifax stands an old gravestone erected to the memory of one Pat Flynn. It bears the following inscription.

When I am dead and in my grave
Please mark the spot with a marble stave
So folks can say, "There he lies,
Poor Pat, who made the rods and flies."

Original rhyming epitaphs being scarce hereabouts, I decided to honour gentle Pat with a few lines of my own.

Well, Pat, I saw your epitaph today
As many a time I've stopped to look before
And, though no fisherman myself, I say
Each time I stop one benediction more
On you who made of split bamboo and twine,
Of feather, fur and fish-deceiving hook
The finest rod that ever cast a line
And prettiest Red Ibis in the book.

Your verse, though unpretentious, rhymes quite well
And scans without a flaw of any size;
Among the other gravestones in the dell
It still attracts the most attentive eyes.
Although you never scaled Olympian slopes
Or saw electric lights spell out your name,
You left behind you what each mortal hopes
To will posterity: your share of fame.

Your small quatrain may surely not be hailed
In literary terms as quite the best.
But, though your marble stave has been assailed
By winds that whistle over Ashburn's crest
And smoke from old Chebucto's reeking mills
Since you went on to streams all starry-spangled,
Your testament's still there to prove your skills:
Four lines unreeled, well-cast, and still untangled.

Dukes, Ducks and Doggerel Ditties

The Duke and the Duck

If a cat can look at a king, surely a duck can quack at a duke. This narrative is built on such a premise, with a few tongue-traps thrown in for readers-aloud.

When Richard, Duke of Dillingham, went riding out one
    day,
A small brown duck confronted him somewhere along the
    way.
Said Duke to duck, "Fly, churlish bird! You stand upon my
    path!
Pray move yourself or next prepare to feel a noble's wrath."
At this the duck inclined her head and halted in her track;
Deferring not, she stood her ground and answered only,
    "Quack."
Enraged, the Duke spurred on his steed and waved his
    dukely dirk.
He cried, "To make duck soup of you would be but simple
    work!"
The duck took little note. In fact she showed a total lack
Of evidence that she had heard, but answered only,
    "Quack."
The path on which this scene took place ran down along a
    dike
That held the sea from farms where grew green cabbage
    and the like.
There, Duke and duck and dirk and dike composed a
    drama tense,
For duck's insouciance was rare and Duke's chagrin
    immense.
With dirk, Duke Dick did swipe full quick at duck on dike
    that day,
And duck said, "Quack," once more as if to signal that
    she'd stay.
The apoplectic Duke did eye his duck opponent there
And said, "Duck, die by dirk of Duke or dike at once
    foreswear!"
The awful scene that next ensued was one which must be
    hid,

For tender souls must not be told what duck to Duke then
   did.
Suffice to say in bed next day Duke lay in anguish sore
Face down; his poor posterior a duckbill bruise-mark wore.
And on a palace window-ledge behind his noble back
Sat something very like a duck, which uttered only,
   "Quack."

Odd Names

Many names carry an extra level of meaning, although not necessarily a very profound one. These three can be considered as examples of a form of diversion usually best confined to the backs of envelopes.

Sir Lester Noyes, a man of poise
And also of gentility,
Thought it a shame his given name
Bespoke no affability.
He shortened it by quite a bit
And now he quite enjoys
The footman's call, when at a ball
The cry rings out: "Les Noyes!"

Young Barbara Dwyer had one desire:
To keep her ancient father
From fear, alarm, concern or harm
(A kind objective, rather).
Thus every day, so people say,
The venerable sire
Remains secure, serene and sure
Protected by Barb Dwyer.

A dog named Hamlet frolics
On the Mellon family grounds,
Result of careless breeding 'midst
The Mellon family hounds.
A Great Dane known as Rowdy
And a collie known as Jane
Were sire and dam of Hamlet;
He's the Mellon collie-Dane.

The Melancholy Newspaper Career of Dickerson Dort

The entreaty, "Just make sure you spell the name right," is usually in vain. Sometimes, though, the journalistic outcome is worse than others.

Dickerson Dort was a hard-working sort
On whose honesty one could depend;
An eager young scribe on the Post-Diatribe,
He was often the fellow they'd send
To amateur plays and Activity Days,
Bazaars and society teas
And Dickerson Dort used to have to report
On such sorts of stories as these.

Now Dickerson's boss was Fiander McFloss,
A very tough fellow indeed;
An editor type of the hard-minded stripe
Who followed the journalist's creed
Which, stated in brief, maintained that the chief
Among rules of the newsperson's trade
Was spelling each name in the story the same
As the subject's own habit obeyed.

But Dickerson Dort fell incredibly short
Of his editor's standard, alack;
His pen had a quirk that affected his work
And finally got him the sack.
He tried to evade such mistakes as he made,
But somehow 'twas always the same
For, try as he might, what he never got right
Was the spelling of anyone's name.

So feckless was he that he went to the tea
Presented by plump Martha Wilde
And left out the 'l' when attempting to spell
Her name in the story he filed.
When Dickerson wrote of the outing by boat
Of the Parish of Scabwell-on-Sea
His syntax would pass, but the Reverend Paul Gass
Was missing his capital 'G'.

The Glee Club of Bray wasn't charmed by the way
Young Dort did his write-up on them:
Miss Farmer, who sang, had a cardiac pang
When a 't' took the place of her 'm'.
And just as inept were the notes that he kept
On a track meet at Camberwell Lea;
When Tennyson Hurd in the road-race came third,
Dort transposed the 'H' and the 'T'.

Dort's job met its end when he had to attend
The amateur musical show
Put on by the staff of O'Flanagan, Braff,
Macomber, Corelli & Crowe.
He wrote a big spread with a two-column head
And the Post ran the story next day.
McFloss was appalled when he read it, and called
"Tell Dort he can pick up his pay!"

Old Ruby McBrum, who was playing the drum
In the ranks of the company band,
Grew crimson with shame when she saw what her name
Had become under Dickerson's hand.
The 'y' seemed to be in the place of the 'c',
Which was dropped; this gave Ruby a jar;
But even worse yet, Dort contrived to forget
In the surname the lower-case 'r'.

The cellist, Horst Shinn, nearly did himself in
When he opened the paper and read
The absolute shame that had come to his name
He felt he'd be better off dead.
Dort lifted his 't', substituting an 'e'
And with it replaced double 'n'
Which made the man tear up his music and swear
He'd not play in public again.

Having lost the support of Fiander, young Dort
Looked out for a suitable job.
He found it, they say, over Hardcastle way
With the firm of DeLorey & Robb
Where he now takes his stand with new tools in his hand
And never a spelling he shirks
As he chisels and chips with a smile on his lips
At the Hardcastle Monument Works.

A Concise History of Halifax

Thomas Raddall tells the story of Halifax and its history in Warden
of The North, *and nobody could tell it better. Recognizing that I'll
never write the best, I set myself the job of writing the shortest
account of the old seaport city. The Indian camps, the ill-fated
expedition of the Duc D'Anville, the founding of the city by Edward
Cornwallis, the command of the garrison by Edward, Duke of Kent
are here. So are the War of 1812 and the prosperity it generated, the
privateer fleet of banker Enos Collins, Joseph Howe's seminal
newspaper career, the discontent with Confederation despite the
railway that came with it. Then there was the traditional slump
between wars, the business boom that came with World War I and
the more literal boom of the devastating Halifax Explosion. From
there we go to the rebuilding of the wrecked North End, another
slump, another war and the overcrowding, the V-E Day riots and
the second, smaller explosion that were part of it. The rest of the
story is the welcome peacetime growth, the bridge links with
Dartmouth and the present great shape that Halifax is in. Not
definitive, but at least, at 66 words, mercifully brief.*

Micmacs banded,
D'Anville stranded,
Corny landed,
Ed commanded.

War-swords glinted,
Collins minted,
Joe Howe printed,
Trade unstinted.

Railroad station
Linked new nation;
Federation
Caused vexation.

Trade eroded,
World War boded,
Troop ships loaded,
Place exploded.

Renovated,
Trade abated,
More war fated,
Town inflated.

V-E brew-up,
Ammo blew up,
Suburbs grew up
Bridges new up.

Now less gritty,
Looking pretty.
Great old city!
End of ditty.

Games with Names

There's no fun like taking a pronunciation that doesn't match the spelling and, with that as a basis, letting your mind run amuck in limerick form. If your mind is of the right twist, these few can be considered a jump-start.

There was an old parson from Reading
Who drank too much punch at a weading.
He chased bride and groom
To their honeymoon room
And blithely set fire to their beading.

There once was a swimmer from Cobh
Who didn't take care where he dobh.
He happened to leap
On a shark, half asleep,
Who woke up and ate him, by Jobh!

A keen treasure-hunter named Pepys
Goes diving for gold in the depys,
But all he can find
Is sea-cucumber rind
Of which he amasses great hepys.

There was a young girl called Colquohoun
Who planned for a wedding in Juquohoun
But after a fight
On the pre-nuptial night,
"Not ever," she said, "is too sooquohoun!"

A lady who lived by the Thames
Adorned all her dresses with games,
At the shoulders and neck
There were pearls by the peck
And rubies were ringed round the hames.

A clever enchantress named Circe
Turned men into swine without mirce
Which creatures she sold
(Or so we are told)
To a pig-farming fellow named Pirce

Doctor Hennigar's Universal Cure

Words and music by Jim Bennet

Doctor Hennigar's Universal Cure

Friday night when I was drinking in the tavern I got
  stinking
And the bouncer took and threw me out the back.
I landed in an awful lump right in the middle of a dump,
And for a moment everything went black.
I was just about to travel when I heard a voice of gravel
Come from somewhere just above my aching head
And I lay in fascination at a wonderful narration;
Let me give you some idea what he said:

Recitative
"My dear friend! Are you troubled with vertigo, headache,
cranial protuberances, sudden chills, neuresthenic debility
or nervous catarrh? Afflicted with ague, chilblains, quinsy
or hallucinatory manifestations? Subject to spasms,
vapours, involuntary micturition, and all other ailments to
which the physiographical configuration is susceptible?
Well, friend, take heart! For I bring you...

Chorus
Doctor Hennigar's Oil of Palm,
Antiphlogistical Mystical Balm,
Physiopathical Medical Bitters and Universal Cure!
Absolutely guaranteed an anodyne for every need,
Effectiveness is absolutely sure.
For the rabies and the scabies and the diaper rash in babies
A prompt alleviation to ensure
Try Doctor Hennigar's Oil of Palm,
Antiphlogistical, Mystical Balm,
Physiopathical Medical Bitters and Universal Cure!"

Verse
I rolled over then to see just who it was addressing me
And there a rotund individual did stand;
He wore a lofty beaver hat, a purple vest, a pink cravat
And held a little bottle in his hand
Which he thrust in my direction for approval and inspection
While exhorting me to seize upon the chance.
And while I read the label Doctor Hennigar was able
To extract the last two dollars from my pants.

Recitative
"A wise selection, my friend! A panacea that has pacified the pulsations of the crowned heads of Europe! The preference of professors and philosophers, a redoubtable remedy among regents, potentates, prelates, presidents and plutocrats; the choice of chemists, apothecaries, formulizers and homeopathic practitioners alike. That unparalleled specific for numberless vexatious and virulent conditions, and winner of gold medals at the Paris, Luxembourg and Brussels exhibitions...

Chorus
Doctor Hennigar's Oil of Palm,
Antiphlogistical Mystical Balm,
Physiopathical Medical Bitters and Universal Cure!
For tremors, constipation and nocturnal ambulation
And other ailments common and obscure;
Taken for astigmatism or for anthropopathism
It's a super-synchronistic cynosure:
Doctor Hennigar's Oil of Palm,
Antiphlogistical Mystical Balm,
Physiopathical Medical Bitters and Universal Cure!"

Verse

When the morning sun came shining on the dump, I lay
  reclining
With a skinny rat reposing on my knee.
I cursed the lousy luck of life, and wondered what to tell
  the wife
And what the form of her reply would be.
Deeper still in my dejection I regained a recollection
Of the vision that disturbed my evening's rest,
Then I rolled on something lumpy, something round and
  hard and bumpy—
'Twas a bottle in the pocket of my vest!

Recitative

And, sure enough, when I withdrew it and examined it in
the rosy glow of sunrise, there, beneath reproductions of
medals from the Paris, Luxembourg and Brussels exhibi-
tions, and the legend, "Patent Pending," in bold-faced
Gothic typescript of the most florid configuration I was able
to discern the following hyperbolic inscription:

Chorus

Doctor Hennigar's Oil of Palm,
Antiphlogistical Mystical Balm,
Physiopathical Medical Bitters and Universal Cure!
For bunions, corns and evening chills
And sundry other human ills
Its palliative properties are pure
For shingles and psoriasis, acute hypochondriasis
A permanent remission to secure
Try Doctor Hennigar's Oil of Palm,
Antiphlogistical Mystical Balm,
Physiopathical Medical Bitters and Universal Cure!

Baited Lines

*Those who do the Times or Manchester Guardian crosswords will
have no trouble finding a catch in the following lines. Mackerel,
squid, turbot or ray: they're all here, and just beneath the surface.*

When Florence Gray came east to stay
With Mack and Perc her brothers,
Her ringing oath she gave to both
She'd never disturb others.
Nor did the pair feel less than fair
This pledge to put Flo under:
She snored so loud 'twould stun a crowd;
Ten choirs she could out-thunder;
No psalm on Sunday, no not one,
Could louder shake a rafter!
The bedlam prey to which fell they
Brought them in no way laughter,
So Perc and Mack ere launching back
Their guest by railway car penned
A cheque to Flo as *quid pro quo*
To dull their cruel spike's sharp end.
Now, readers, hark and try to mark
The meaning: words had never
More hidden codes in fishy modes.
Just dabble (and be clever).
No winner's cup will you hold up
For seeking fish so fine;
Withal I but will show (guess what)
One fish on every line.

A Touching Tale in Which We Learn the Progress of a Tender Fern

The wild fiddlehead fern beats broccoli, and rivals asparagus as a gourmet green vegetable. Along with skipping-ropes and hopscotch, it's a certain sign of spring. Prime source of the little coiled morsels is Nova Scotia's sister province of New Brunswick, in honour of which I include one of the most strained rhymes of my career.

As dawn's taper lights the sun's wick
O'er the woodlands of New Brunswick,
In the soil there comes a whirring
As of pteridophyte stirring;
'Tis a fern in peat well bedded,
Slim of stalk and fiddle-headed.
Soon its curly locks a-borning
Meet the bright New Brunswick morning.
When it's grown a few short inches
It will feel the pulls and pinches
Of the fiddlehead fanatic
Salivating and ecstatic
Whose enchantment will be utter
When it's steamed and served with butter.

Asleep in the Deep: Some Nautical Epitaphs

There are many ways to meet Davy Jones. I quote from the headstones from some who dropped in on him.

Friend, shed a teardrop for good Captain Mitton;
Steamed out of Halifax bound for Great Britain.
Turned hard a-starboard instead of to port,
Rendering life both unhappy and short.

Down in Davy Jones's locker
Lies Commander Grubb.
Always best to close the hatches
When you dive your sub.

Say a prayer for Captain Bundy;
Sailed a freighter from the Fundy.
Couldn't find his tidal table.
Vita breve. Heed the fable.

Late lamented Larry Lawrence
Didn't stay afloat.
Never, never hunt for swordfish
From a rubber boat.

No more on the North West Arm
Frolics Sally Skimming.
Didn't know the sewer flushed
Where she did her swimming.

Talkin' Nautical's So Nice

Equinox magazine once published an article on the late schooner builder and sailor David Stevens in which the author describes Mr. Stevens as shouting the order to "hoist the fo'c'sle." Obviously, he shouted no such thing; the fo'c'sle (or forecastle) occupies the entire forward portion of the vessel. But between fo'c'sle and foresail, bilge and binnacle, one of the landlubber's chief delights is getting the chance to talk hearty, mateys.

Hoist up the fo'c'sle and let go the keel,
Slack off the sextant, avast!
Batten the boom vang and shake out the wheel,
Lash the ship's head to the mast.
Port the companionway, starboard the stays,
Pipe down the binnacle light,
Brail up the capstan and see how she lays,
Sling aft the bows in a bight.
Lower the bulkheads and coil down the rail,
Galley-stove gimbals let run,
Make fast the transom, we're off for a sail
And talking like tars is such fun.

For it's haul away handsomely, scupper your yard,
Lay aloft into the pumps,
Hatches and deadeyes to windward, and hard,
A lubber the last one who jumps!
Ship ahoy, cast off and bilges aweigh,
Sound the main halyard and block,
Cheerily, mateys, we're sailing today
And talking like sailors all talk.
And when we return from our cruise on the bay
We certainly hope that no jokes'll
Be made of the way we left harbour today
By hoisting away on our fo'c'sle.

Romantic Antics

Cape Breton Romance

The euphonious, if lengthy, names of Cape Bretoners are functional as well as beautiful. You can find areas where there are hundreds of Campbells, dozens of John Campbells. But when the name goes on to specify John Roderick Donald Campbell, you'll get the one you're looking for. (It's also nice, when you've got eight or nine children, to be able to name every one of them after their mother or father.)

Rory John Angus Dan Alec MacIsaac
And Mary Elizabeth Josephine Hay
Came from (respectively) close to Whycocomagh
And from a village down Washabuck way.
Rory John Angus was blessed with the Gaelic;
Mary Elizabeth Josephine, too,
Spoke with the lilt of the far-away islands,
Tones of the Hebrides falling like dew.

Rory John Angus Dan Alec MacIsaac
Went to a ceilidh one long-ago night,
Walked over mountainside, meadow and marshes,
Bathed in the moon's early-gathering light.
Mary Elizabeth came in a wagon
Drawn by her father's slow-plodding old mare,
Stopped at the house of the hosts of the party
Just at the moment MacIsaac got there.

Eyelashes lowered, the girl stood demurely;
Gaping and gazing, the lad stood in awe.
Instantly smitten, the one with the other,
Too shy to speak but too bold to withdraw,
Awkwardly, ardently, Rory and Mary,
There, with the Cape Breton moonlight above,
Silently planted the seeds of a union
Destined for decades of Cape Breton love.

Rory John Angus Dan Alec MacIsaac
And Mary Elizabeth Josephine Hay
Mothered and fathered a fine fold of children
As the long years since that night slipped away.
One is called Angus, another called Mary,
Rory, Elizabeth, Josephine too;
Twins, John and Dan, and wee Alec (the youngest)
Round out the rolls of their Cape Breton crew.

Plentiful playmates live close to the household:
Duncan and Flora and Archie and Ann,
James and Fiona, Rod, Kenzie and Jeannie,
Daughters and sons of a neighbouring clan,
Youngsters with roots in that very same ceilidh
Where part of the very same spirited crowd
Were Duncan James Archie Rod Kenzie MacDonald
And Jeannie Fiona Ann Flora MacLeod.

Love, Nova Scotia Style

*To be able to read this ditty aloud and get all the rhymes right first
time around is the hallmark of the true Bluenose, born or adopted.
Others may get the idea from context. Either way, checking out the
pronunciations with the residents of these places could make for a
very pleasant tour of the province.*

A carpenter from Necum Teuch
Packed up a hammer and a seuch;
Built a house in Musquodoboit,
Made it strong so none could roboit.
Wooed a girl from Gabarus,
Liked her looks but found her lus.
Found another in Ben Eionn,
Turned around and she was goinn.
Met a girl from Havre Bouche,
Found her fun, but rather pouche.
Dropped her for a lass from Minas
Much preferred for quiet shinas.
Soon a parson from Port Joli
Made them man and wife, by goli!
Spent a week in Port Mouton
On a pleasant honeymon;
Home by way of old Nictaux
To live by hammer and by saux.

The Swinimication of Polly Pulsifer

If you're fond of games like Fun with Names, Nova Scotia is a perfect playground. Start with a surname ending with 'er', such as Rhodenizer, do a quick back formation to get "one who rhodenizes" and then invent your own definition of the verb. It can get pretty bizarre.

One lovely night beside the shore
(Thus starts this true confession)
Young Polly Pulsifer gave o'er
Her dearest-held possession.
The boy who robbed her of the prize
And left her sad but wiser?
A trawlerman with roving eyes:
Young Andy Rhodenizer.

Now Andy bragged to every lad
Who trod the deck beside him
Of all the selfish fun he'd had
When Polly Pulsified him.
And she, with tearful eyes and wet
Her girlfriends all apprised
Of how she'd wept with deep regret
Since she'd been Rhodenized.

But Billy Swinimer, a boy
Of scallop-fishing faction
With one punch ended Andy's joy
And put him out of action.
Bill asked for pretty Polly's hand,
Demurrals proved quite minimal;
And now she wears his wedding band
Her life is sweet and Swinimal.

Hermione Zwicker

Words and music by Jim Bennet

moderate

A   E7   E7

Let me sing of a mai - den from Blue Rocks, Down old No - va Sco - tia's South

A   A   E7

Shore. Where the o - cean con - ceals quite a few rocks, That have

E7   A   F#m

wrecked pas - sing ships by the score. Her name was Her - mi - on - e

C#m   F#m   C#m

Zwi - cker, Her Pa kept the Clam Is - land light. And it

F#m   B7

ne - ver would fal - ter or fli - cker, When he turned up the beam ev' - ry

E7   A

night. And ev - ry ten se - conds, the lens it ro - ta - ted, (By

E7   A   D

ca - bles well weigh - ted). And thus in - di - ca - ted To 'sai - lors the way past the

A   E7   A

shoals that they ha - ted. As - sur - ing them things were all right.

Hermione Zwicker

Verse
Let me sing of a maiden from Blue Rocks
Down old Nova Scotia's South Shore,
Where the ocean conceals quite a few rocks,
That have wrecked passing ships by the score.
Her name was Hermione Zwicker;
Her Pa kept the Clam Island light,
And it never would falter or flicker
When he turned up the beam every night.

Chorus
And ev'ry ten seconds the lens it rotated
(By cables well weighted) and thus indicated
To sailors the way past the shoals that they hated,
Assuring them things were all right.

Verse
Such a belle was Hermione Zwicker,
A vision of charm and delight,
All the lovesick young men grew lovesicker
When they gazed at her beauty so bright.
They rowed out to Hermione Zwicker,
A diff'rent young man every night—
Cuddled up on the loveseat of wicker
On the porch of the Clam Island Light.

Chorus
And ev'ry ten seconds it flashed in their faces
Revealing the places that still bore the traces
Of kisses, near-misses and half-loosened laces,
Shown up by the Clam Island light.

Verse
They gave up Hermione Zwicker;
They rowed off to left and to right
Till it seemed sure that no one would pick her
As long as her Pa kept the light.
Then one evening, Hermione Zwicker
She welcomed a fellow named White.
One hand held a pint of good liquor
And one held a slingshot some tight. *(Sound of breaking glass)*

Chorus
Then ev'ry ten seconds was like ev'ry other,
The darkness concealed them from Father and Mother,
While out on the bay vessels rammed one another!
But the lovers were doing all right.

Verse
She once was Hermione Zwicker,
But now she's Hermione White.
She's grown a bit older and thicker,
And she and her man keep the light.
The two seldom quarrel or bicker,
Their friends say that they never fight.
In fact, they're as quick, if not quicker,
To head for the loveseat each night.

Chorus
Then every ten seconds, the light wakes up seven
Wee babies who all start to howl to high heaven
Till he gets out his slingshot at ten past eleven
And puts out the Clam Island light.

The Luckless Lot of Aloysius McCarthy

*Betty Jean Ferguson of Halifax was crowned Miss Canada in 1948,
and for a year thousands of Haligonians burst with pride (and, in
the case of ardent adolescent swains, puppy-love). This is the story of
a feckless fellow who never recovered, and followed generations of
Misses down the line of succession with never a hit.*

My name's Aloysius McCarthy,
And Halifax City's my home.
I like it quite well; it's a good place to dwell
And I've seldom been tempted to roam.
But early in life I developed
A passion that took a firm hold
For girls who wear gowns and magnificent crowns
And sashes block-lettered in gold.

It started right here in my birthplace,
This passion for girls of acclaim
When one Betty Jean was elected as queen
In a contest of country-wide fame.
Miss Canada! That's what they crowned her,
And Halifax youths by the score
Were thrilled from afar when they heard such a star
Was the Ferguson girl from next door.

I never quite managed to meet her,
But still I was faithful and proud;
I'd manfully vie for Miss Canada's eye
From my place at the back of the crowd.
The longing she started within me
I've tried ever since to assuage:
If not Betty Jean, then what other queen
Could I sweep off her feet and her stage?

With ill-hidden anticipation
I waited for Natal Day's date.
Miss Halifax might be the queen who'd delight
To accept me as regent and mate.
I waited along her parade-route;
Her royal float grandly swept by
But, try as I might, I was unable quite
To attract her imperial eye.

Miss French Village Labour Day Picnic;
Miss Lobster of Liverpool Bay;
Miss Salt Herring Feast of Jeddore West and East;
Each one turned me down in her way.
Miss Volunteer Fire Department
Of Middle Branch Indian Brook;
Miss Candlepin Bowler, Miss Junior Log Roller,
Miss Baked Bean of Little Skidook.

Miss Cabbage of Ironbound Island,
Miss Hodge-Podge, Miss Raspberry Pie,
Miss Cape Island Boat and Miss Herring Net Float
All spurned such a fellow as I.
And so did Miss Peggy's Cove Lighthouse,
Miss Hand-Crafted Quilt of New Ross,
Miss Lift-Top Commode and Miss Corduroy Road,
Miss Homebrew and Miss Irish Moss.

I hankered for Miss Musquodoboit,
Miss Pugwash Potato Day too;
I plighted my suit to Miss Hobnail Boot
And also Miss Longliner Crew.
Miss Fish-Meal and By-Products shunned me,
Miss Cranberry told me to scram;
Miss Lumber Camp Cook wouldn't give me a look,
No more would Miss Blueberry Jam.

Of all the Miss-This-That-and-Others
That might have accepted my suit
There's never been one who even in fun
Encouraged my luckless pursuit.
So I'm moving to Newfoundland shortly
And there my whole future will be,
For in Fortune Bay, where I'm planning to stay,
Miss Fortune is waiting for me.

Doris Corkum

*This is a highly unlikely narrative to the extent that no Chester girl
of my acquaintance ever became a belly-dancer in a travelling circus.
But the possibility, however scant, presented an opportunity to try
out an unusual rhyme scheme and a few little-used rhymes. Circus?
Ghurkas? Purkis? Read on—aloud, if you dare.*

Doris Corkum was a girly
Who showed great ambition early;
With her girlfriend, Shirley Perley,
She ran off and joined the circus.
Met a barker, Curly Purkis,
Drawing crowds for dancing Ghurkas.
Billed as Fatima Sarducci,
Shirley trained a poodle poochie;
Doris did the hoochie-koochie.
Tired of circus hurly-burly,
Shirley Perley first grew surly,
Then betrayed the burly Curly:
Stole the till and fled for Chester
And her faithful boyfriend Lester
(He of oilskin and sou'wester).
Meanwhile, burly Curly Purkis,
Doris Corkum and the Ghurkas,
Plus assorted circus workers
Followed Shirl in agitation,
Caught her at the Chester station.
What a massive confrontation!
Silly, surly Shirley Perley,
Ghurkas, circus workers, Curly,
In a hellish hurly-burly
Making scenes so loud and awful,
So unruly and unlawful.
To go on would be a jawful.

Pubnico

Words and music by Jim Bennet

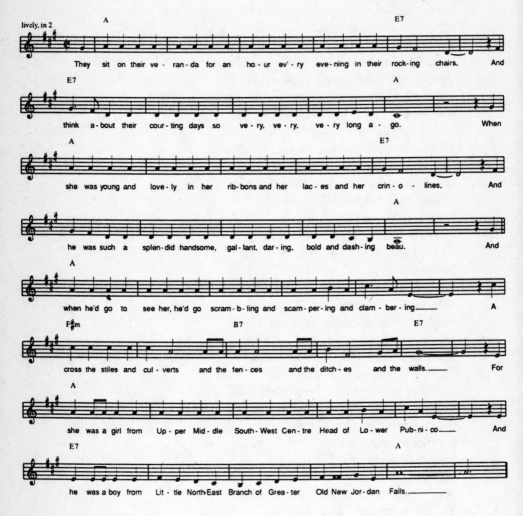

Pubnico

They sit on their veranda for an hour every evening in their
   rocking-chairs
And think about their courting days so very, very, very
   long ago
When she was young and lovely in her ribbons and her
   laces and her crinolines
And he was such a splendid, handsome, gallant, daring,
   bold and dashing beau.
And when he'd go to see her, he'd go scrambling and
   scampering and clambering
Across the stiles and culverts and the fences and the ditches
   and the walls,
For she was a girl from Upper Middle Southwest Centre
   Head of Lower Pubnico
And he was a boy from Little Northeast Branch of Greater
   Old New Jordan Falls.

They simpered and they whimpered and they murmured
   and they whispered and they rolled their eyes,
They huddled and they cuddled and they bundled and they
   snuggled and they kissed.
And she would sip upon a rather dainty little glass of
   cherry cordial
And he would chew upon a somewhat larger little plug of
   Pictou Twist.
He took her to the quilting bees, the husking bees, the
   dances and the gatherings;
He took her to the suppers and the picnics and the parties
   and the balls;
And some were held in Upper Middle Southwest Centre
   Head of Lower Pubnico,
And some were held in Little Northeast Branch of Greater
   Old New Jordan Falls.

Her relatives were loath to see her leave the ancient family seat in Pubnico
And his to have them settle down in Jordan Falls were
    equally as keen,
So they measured off the distance as the crow might fly
    from Jordan Falls to Pubnico
And built their little cottage just exactly half the distance in
    between.
And now on their veranda they sit rocking, nodding,
    knitting and remembering;
They listen to the herring gull that dips and wheels and
    screams and squawks and squalls
As the sun goes down on Upper Middle Southwest Centre
    Head of Lower Pubnico,
And the moon comes up on Little Northeast Branch of
    Greater Old New Jordan Falls.

Nova Scotia Diet

Nova Scotia Diet

Nova Scotia Diet

This song worried my grandson Benjamin when he was four years old. I have had to assure him that he doesn't have to like every one of the seafoods listed to qualify as a Nova Scotian—being born in Annapolis Royal and fond of haddock is sufficient. Similar dispensation comes free to readers with the purchase of this book.

Verse
You can tell a Nova Scotian
By the fragrance of the ocean,
For they always wear the perfume
Of the North Atlantic spray.
But, if you can't seem to smell 'em,
There's another way to tell 'em,
For you'll always know a Bluenose
By his diet right away. What do we eat?

Chorus
We eat pickled herring,
Oysters when we're daring,
And we often take and bake a hake,
For that's a dandy dish.
To make chowder good for gulpin'
Throw in ev'rything but sculpin
And you ain't a Nova Scotian
If you don't like fish.

Verse
What we eat until we're busting
Most Albertans find disgusting,
For it seems salt cod's upsetting
To the dainty western tum.
And, with faces hard and stony,
They say, "Herring's too durn bony!"
But there's nothing for dissolving bones
Like Nova Scotia rum. So,

Chorus
We eat cod cheeks, cod tongues,
(Even though they're odd tongues)
Fish sticks and Digby chicks
As dainty as you wish.
We eat flatfish like the flounder
And some others that are rounder,
And you ain't a Nova Scotian
If you don't like fish.

Verse
You won't find no haddock fillets
In them Manitoba skillets,
And away out in Saskatchewan
They don't know fish from beans.
No one in Red River Valley
Can tell scallops from tomalley
And you'll get no clams or salmon
With your dandelion greens. But us,

Chorus
We eat finnan haddie
(Good for lass or laddie)
And a smoked eel will make you feel
Like dancing a schottische.
We serve up solomon gundy
Twenty-seven ways from Sunday
And you ain't a Nova Scotian
If you don't like fish.

Verse
Now, lest there should be a mix-up
There's just one thing I should fix up,
For there's some that can't tell us
From Newfoundlanders tried and true.
We eat capelin, cod and kippers
But we don't eat seal flippers,
And that's how you tell the difference,
'Cause the Newfoundlanders do!

Chorus
We just eat mackerel, pollock,
Never give you colic
When you wash down your tuna
With a little drink of swish.
We like a mess of shad roe,
Tommycod or gaspereaux.
You ain't a Nova Scotian
By the holy land o' Goshen,
And you never seen the ocean
If you don't like fish!

Oysters of the Maritimes

Nutritionists will tell you that oysters are rich in iron. Dinner-table philosophers will tell you that it was a brave soul who first ate one. I'll tell you that there is no leisure pursuit as rewarding as leaning over the transom of a dinghy in a cove of the beautiful Bras d'Or Lakes, reaching into the mud for fresh, wild appetizers of the mollusc family. New Brunswick and Prince Edward Island have similarly succulent harvests fit for half-shell, Rockefeller or stew treatment—but keep your greedy little fingers off the cultivated ones or risk the wrath of an underwater farmer!

Bedded snug in Buctouche Bay
In her quiet bivalve way
She's a morsel plump and tender,
Though it's hard to tell her gender
Nestled in her calcite cloister:
Lovely little Buctouche oyster!

In the Gulf's caressing tide,
Spat in millions by her side,
Toothsome, succulent, sedate
In her limestone armour plate;
None is sweeter, plumper, moister.
Smooth, delicious Malpeque oyster.

In the waters of Bras d'Or
Sleeping sound with scarce a snore,
Full of dimpled delectation
Under careful cultivation,
Disinclined to brawl or roister:
Delicate Cape Breton oyster.

Dulse

Biologists call it rhodata palmata. *The tasteless call it a delicacy.*
But dulse is firmly established as a seaweed snack in our Bluenose
society, thanks to the encouragement of the people of Grand Manan,
an island in the Bay of Fundy, who harvest, dry and sell the
wretched stuff. If offered a bag of it, try to find some alternative.

Some of us like it and some of us hate it.
I'm found in the ranks of the latter.
To call the stuff foul is to quite overrate it
And, friend, that's an end to the matter.
It looks like red leather all torn into rags
And covered with mildew and mold
That's been over-salted and stuffed into bags
Then left to go brittle and old.
No substance on earth is as sure at first taste
A civilized soul to repulse
As that rubbery, salty, inedible waste
That Grand Manan people call dulse.
If you, unlike me, may a dulse-lover be
Though taste we may not be the same in,
We'll get along fine: you eat your share plus mine
And I'll eat the bag that it came in.

The Divine Mission of Abercrombie Gwynne

Some religions forbid alcohol, some bar tea and coffee, some disallow morsels of various meats. Is it too much to suppose that a zealous cleric might get the idea that abstention from one or another type of pickle might tip the balance on the Day of Judgement?

Ponder now the fate of parson Abercrombie Gwynne
Who held that eating bread-and-butter pickles was a sin.
On other points of doctrine he was middle-of-the-road
With no divergent practices (or none, at least, that showed).
But in this one respect he was inordinately firm,
A fact that made parishioners and presbytery squirm,
And many necks in synod felt an apprehensive prickle
When Abercrombie Gwynne discussed the bread-and-
   butter-pickle.
"It is," he'd intone piously, "degenerate and lewd
To use a sliced-up cucumber in vinegar as food;
A practice quite intolerable, well beyond the pale
And solid grounds for excommunication (if not jail).
No greater sin, in fact, can I conceive of, much less utter,
Than swallowing of pickles of the genus bread-and- butter."
His peroration over, he'd invariably quit
And turn to other subjects with both tolerance and wit
While his astounded audience, still taken quite aback,
Would wonder at the cause of this anomalous attack.
For Abercrombie Gwynne was never prompted to condemn
The gherkin or the garlic dill; he never mentioned them.
Hot piccalilli likewise he would tacitly allow,
And mango chutney relishes and green tomato chow.
Your potted sweet pimento, pickled watermelon rind,
Your artichokes in vinegar he didn't seem to mind,
But bread-and-butter pickles were an ever-growing source
Of his hearty disapproval and pejorative discourse.
In time he grew obsessive and his fellows grew dismayed
As more and more allusions to his quirk were daily made,
For on his church's notice board, most every other week,
Among such subject matter as *Turn Thou the Other Cheek*,
The Missionary Message or *The Church From Pole to Pole*

Appeared, writ large, *The Bread-and-Butter-Pickle And Your Soul.*
At length his congregation shrank to half its former size,
The elders of the vestry met and smote their sombre thighs;
A delegation of concern was chosen to begin
A bread-and-butter dialogue with Abercrombie Gwynne.
Their visits unsuccessful, the committee made report
And recommended pastoral impeachment of a sort.
The congregation voted their unanimous assent,
And soon on vestry letterhead this chilling message went:
"Dear Pastor: We, your flock, can now no longer overlook
Your constant deviations from the tenets of the book.
Your usual attendance, sir, has dwindled to a trickle
In ratio inverse to talk of bread-and-butter pickle.
Thus, sir, you may consider this your notice to vacate
Your posting and your parsonage effective from this date.
Yours truly, Board of Elders, Funds and Superannuation.
P.S. Enclosed is final cheque adjusted for vacation."
So now Gwynne sets out daily with a walking-stick of birch
From his Anti-Bread-and-Butter Pickle New Reformist
    Church
With reverential air of utter sanctity and grace,
A smile of benediction on his New Reformist face.
Then all the market-keepers on his customary route
Aware of his eccentric predilection by repute,
Will rush to take the bread-and-butter pickles from the shelf
Lest Abercrombie Gwynne should take the job upon himself
And swing his fearful walking-stick like swift-descending
    sickle
Against the evil presence of the bread-and-butter pickle.

Swish

One of the favourite types of recycling in Atlantic Canada is swish-making. It's based on the knowledge that when a rum-barrel is 'empty,' it really isn't. There's enough of the good stuff soaked into the wood to provide many the jolly moment. The technology is simple: one barrel, one kettle. The rest is rambunctious (and most likely illegal).

Start off with a barrel that's been lately full of rum
(Admittedly quite difficult to borrow, beg or bum,
But a sympathetic shipper or distiller may take heed
And let you have the oaken raw material you need).

Then you pull the bung out, place the barrel on your lawn
And fill a good-sized water kettle up and put it on;
When the water's boiling, bring it out and pour it in.
Replace the bung in bung-hole and you're ready to begin.

You thump the keg and bump it and you roll it down the
    street,
You kick it and you cuff it, alternating hands and feet,
You straddle it and ride it like a little oaken horse
And then you turn it over and go once more round the
    course.

Then unbung it where you've flung it and pour out a little
    drink.
Count seven, turn around and choke, then shudder, wheeze
    and blink,
And when you come around again you try another tot,
And if the same thing happens, friend, then swish is what
    you've got.

Mahone Bay

The town of Mahone Bay lies at the head of the bay of that ilk—a place of widow's walks, gingerbread trim and church spires. Its prosperity, born in times of lumber and fishing barons, is maintained these days by the quaintness industry: tearooms, potters, pewterers and bakeshops by the dozens make it a must for those who find innocent delight in such attractions.

Once the haunt of merchant princes,
Now of ladies in blue rinses,
Thither often who repair
First to take the bracing air
Then the bracing tea to sup
From the dainty Wedgewood cup
(Or the Oriental copy)
At Ye Tea-and-Crumpet Shoppe.
Afterwards they keenly seek
Pewter, pine and quaint antique
Which to buy they're rather prone
In the shops of old Mahone.
Merchant princes of today
Close their eyes each night and say,
"Thank you, Lord, for sending patrons
In the form of blue-haired matrons."

Cape Breton Tea

Forget your lemon slice, put away that tea-cozy and send a red alert
to your stomach-lining: here comes a mug of the high-test!

First you need a kitchen stove with polished iron top.
Then a bubbling kettle that you don't allow to stop.
Then some Orange Pekoe (for no other kind will do)
And a tinware vessel where the stuff can sit and stew.

When it's getting strong enough (in maybe half an hour)
To eat the plating off the spoon, you'll know it's gaining
  power.
If you drop a nail in and the nail doesn't sink
You'll know the tea is closer to a cup that's fit to drink.

Simmer it a little, and for every cup you pour,
You add some tea and water, then you add a little more.
Eighty-five cups later, with the shadows growing deep,
Your tea is at its best for having had some time to steep.

With a final cup you go contented to your bed
With warmly sloshing stomach and with slightly buzzing
  head
To lie in peaceful pleasure from your cares and worries free
To dream about tomorrow and tomorrow's pot of tea.

Digby Chicks

If lightly smoked salmon slices are at the top of the delicacy scale,
surely Digby Chicks define the other end. But salty, smoky and bony
though they may be, we have our uses for them!

'Twixt stones and sticks and Digby chicks
The wise don't choose in haste.
Whoever picks the stones and sticks
To munch, has better taste.
Sliced leather-thin and salt as sin,
With fringe of prickly bone,
They're no fit feast for man nor beast,
And best are left alone.
But if you must try chicks or bust
I'll tell you how it's done.
You put them near a jug of beer
And gently nibble one;
In texture it will seem a bit
Like well-used welcome mat.
The taste, you'll find, will call to mind
The sweatband of a hat
That's been well-brined and tacked behind
The backhouse for a year
Then once more soaked in salt and smoked
And stacked beneath a pier
Until it's ripe as some dead snipe
That's hung until forgotten—
By which I may be judged to say
Particularly rotten.
But if you're game and have no shame
You'll try another bite;
And though a third may seem absurd,
You possibly just might.
By now your tongue is like the bung
Of some old herring puncheon
And you may wish some other fish
Had been your choice for luncheon.
But then with cheer you spot the beer
Which all this time has beckoned
And in one pass you drain your glass

Close followed by a second.
Ah! sweet relief! An end to grief.
You grab the chilly jug
And tip it up; you slurp, you sup,
You swallow chug-a-lug.
You drain each drop without a stop
In case your thirst should worsen,
And once you've quaffed the foamy draft
You'll be a wiser person.
You've learned the tricks of Digby chicks,
The greatest of whose uses
Is as a mere excuse for beer
(For those who need excuses.)

Lunenburg Pudding

There is said to be in Lunenburg County a certain tendency to
haunch, paunch and jowl, euphemistically referred to by old-timers
as a "county figure." If this is so, there is every excuse: the famous
Dutch Oven Cookbook is full of reasons for roundness, from salt
cod and pork scraps to Solomon Gundy. But at the head of my
personal menu are those plump and pungent puddings and sausages
that crown a heap of hot sauerkraut as nothing else can.

Lunenburg pudding,
The black or the white,
Is stuffed in a casing
And tied nice and tight;
While Lunenburg sausage,
In similar fashion,
Is ground to a fare-thee-well,
Spiced with a passion,
Jammed in its skin
Till it threatens to burst,
For in Lunenburg County
Their best is their wurst.
But people who thrive
On this Lunenburg fare
Grow round in proportion
To meals that are square;
And lovers of pudding
May grow, for their sins,
To emulate sausages
Stuffed in their skins.

In Praise of
Bluenose Ways

Thick o' Fog

Words and music by Jim Bennet

jig rhythm **Verse:**

There was a man from Lu - nen burg Whose wife was ve - ry plain. Her face would stop an eight day clock. A trol - ley or a train. Of all the girls in Lu - nen - burg he thought he picked the belle. But the mor - ning he got mar - ried it was kind of hard to tell. In the

Chorus:

fog, thick o' fog. This North At - lan - tic wea - ther is - n't fit for man nor dog. Through the mur - ky mists that blind us And the va - pours that en - wind us, Come and see us (if you can find us) in the fog.

Thick o' Fog

There was a man from Lunenburg
Whose wife was very plain;
Her face would stop an eight-day clock,
A trolley or a train.
Of all the girls in Lunenburg
He thought he'd picked the belle,
But the morning he got married
It was kinda hard to tell...

Chorus
In the fog, thick o' fog,
This North Atlantic weather
Isn't fit for man nor dog.
Through the murky mists that blind us
And the vapours that enwind us
Come and see us (if you can find us) in the fog.

Verse
A mountain climber started out
One damp and dismal day,
To climb up Dauphinee Mountain
Down by old St. Margaret's Bay.
The weather made it hard to know
Just when he ought to stop,
And he went and climbed a hundred feet
Above the mountain top...

Chorus
In the fog, thick o' fog,
This North Atlantic weather
Isn't fit for man nor dog.
Through the murky mists that blind us
And the vapours that enwind us
Come and see us (if you can find us) in the fog.

Verse
Now, Captain Billy Corkum
Of the tugboat *Dainty Bess*
Went out to give assistance
To a schooner in distress.
He threw a line and steamed for home
But, when the fog did thin,
He saw that it was Sambro Island
He was towin' in...

Chorus
In the fog, thick o' fog,
This North Atlantic weather
Isn't fit for man nor dog.
Through the murky mists that blind us
And the vapours that enwind us
Come and see us (if you can find us) in the fog.

Verse
Now, an outhouse beats a lighthouse
As a navigation aid
(Or so says Skipper Tanner
Of the *Aspotogan Maid*).
And, when the weather's thick,
He's got a point there, I suppose:
You can always find your way back home
By followin' your nose...

Chorus
In the fog, thick o' fog,
This North Atlantic weather
Isn't fit for man nor dog.
Through the murky mists that blind us
And the vapours that enwind us
Come and see us (if you can find us) in the fog.

Faint Praise for Winter Days

This work is as much an exercise in a novel rhyme scheme as a complaint about the freezing goop that makes walking less than a pleasure and more than a penitence in the midwinter Maritimes.

When winter's worst is here:
Jan., triple-curst and drear
Or Feb., ice-rimmed, grey-skied,
We go numb-limbed, dull-eyed.
We suffer sore and get
To very core beset
By stuff that Job, poor lad,
To drag his robe ne'er had
Through which; in Bible-land
No ditch, you'll understand,
Did ever hold a jot
Of such a cold, wet lot;
And though his boils were sore,
Our winter's toils are more
Than even he'd forbear
Without the need to swear
At that confounded mush
Called slush.

The Little White House

There is nothing more redolent of nostalgia (well, redolent, anyway)
than the backyard privy. It's a subject irresistible to a doggerel
versifier—even one whose only experience of a two-holer was during
childhood vacations in an old Cape Cod served by outdoor plumbing.

Long years ago in country days when I was just a tad,
The cast iron kitchen pump was all the plumbing that we
　　had,
And 'way out back behind the house there ran a crooked
　　path
That reached the outdoor bathroom where you couldn't
　　take a bath.

Two seats of softwood out there
And an atmosphere so rich and rare,
Where the old Eaton's catalogue lay on the floor
In that little white house with the moon on the door.

'Most every day we'd visit there when nature's call would
　　come.
One hole was made for little folks and one for Dad and
　　Mum;
And there we'd sit and ruminate while bluetail flies would
　　buzz.
Ah, friends, that peaceful moment seemed the best there
　　ever was:

Reading the catalogue through,
Then we'd tear out a back page or two;
And perhaps you'll recall what we wanted them for
In that little white house with the moon on the door.

When summer's warm caressing breezes left us in the fall,
Our combination underwear would complicate each call;
And what about the Hallowe'en we laughed until we cried
When goblins tipped it over with Aunt Isobel inside!

And who could forget Cousin Joel,
So skinny he slipped down the hole
And was buried in shame till a quarter past four
In that little white house with the moon on the door.

The years have brought prosperity, Dame Fortune has been
    good;
My haunches now no longer know the feel of honest wood.
But though I sit on marble seats 'midst chromium and tile,
Each time I go, I close my eyes, and memory makes me
    smile.

Yes, in my mind I go back
To that dear little white-shingled shack
And I'd give all I own just to sit there once more
In that little white house with the moon on the door.

A Nose by Any Other Name Just Ain't as Sweet

Bluenose: a soubriquet worn by Nova Scotians since the glorious Age of Sail and, like the Mary Celeste, *one of the enduring mysteries of the sea. Where did the nickname come from? We have no definitive answers, only a few educated guesses; and even the experts endlessly quibble about those. But one thing we all agree on: it's a name to be proud of.*

Who knows how Bluenose became what they call us?
How did the nickname's arrival befall us?
Some people say the historic connection
Came from potatoes with bluish complexion
Brought to a boil in a cast-iron pot
And eaten with herring both hearty and hot.

Others say Bluenose refers to the hue
Of a fog-sniffer's nose frozen permanent blue;
Not a condition unknown, to be sure,
In deepwater sailors who had to endure
The wild winds of winter in northerly climes
Aboard the windjammers of long-ago times.

These explanations are all that we've got,
And one may explain what the other may not
Concerning our nasal and colourful name.
It makes little difference. To us it's the same
As Taffy to Welshman or Limey to Brit;
It's ours, and we wear it regardless of fit.

From Meat Cove to Yarmouth each toddler of two knows
Full well he or she is a two-year-old Bluenose;
Cherish it, cousins: a thing of our own.
A name to be worn by the chosen alone
And each Nova Scotian, wherever he goes
Ought to value his name as he values his nose.

The Lovely LaHave

*To the discerning motorist, yachtsman, picnicker or painter, there's
no river in Nova Scotia (or anywhere else) more beautiful than the
LaHave. Do those who live along those scenic banks fully appreciate
the value of their surroundings? You bet!*

In Lunenburg County a river there flows
Of which you'll permit me to rave:
Between grassy banks where the cabbage plant grows
Runs ever the lovely LaHave.

From rustic New Germany's rural renown
It rolls from its hinterland source.
Between the abutments of Bridgewater town
It makes its meandering course.

Past dairy and ferry-wharf, foundry and fort,
Past fishery, boatyard and mill,
Past peaceable scenes of the pastoral sort
It runs (as the best rivers will).

The people who live on its beautiful banks,
(The Conrads and Crouses and Youngs)
Are rather inclined to give Providence thanks
At the top of their Lunenburg lungs

Whenever they look at that part of the earth
That God in munificence gave
Those few of sufficiently fortunate birth
To grow up beside the LaHave.

And those of us who in some less lovely place
Have had the ill-fortune to dwell
May thank the good Conrads of eminent grace,
The Youngs and the Crouses as well,

Not to mention each Taylor, each Hebb and each Pentz,
Each Oxner, each Hirtle and Nauss,
All prominent people of practical sense
And seldom unfriendly or cross,

For welcoming warmly the wandering kind
Who seek the relief that they crave
Upon the old byways that gracefully wind
Alongside the lovely LaHave.

The story is told of a Conrad who went
To stand at the Gateway of Pearl
His four score and ten having slowly been spent
Where soft LaHave eddies uncurl;

He spoke to old Peter, the gatekeeper saint;
His words of assessment were grave:
"If you'd plant a few cabbage and touch up your paint,
This place could be like the LaHave!"

How Joggins Kept its Name

Ever wonder how mapmakers react when they come across an unlikely name? I did, and came up with a fanciful conception of what Rand and McNally might have thought when they stumbled across the name Joggins, Nova Scotia.

Rand and McNally (cartographer chaps,
Surveyors of land and purveyors of maps)
Were sitting around with some time on their hands
After running up sketches of various lands
When Rand to McNally said, "Mac, lookit here:
A village called Joggins; how frightfully queer!"

To Rand said McNally, "Why, Randy old scout,
That's certainly strange, as you've just pointed out.
Now why in the name of my sainted aunt's hat
Would anyone ever call any place that?"
Said Rand to McNally, "I really don't know
Whatever possessed them to name the place so.

"Strange names seldom widen a mapmaker's eyes,
But these Nova Scotians walk off with the prize.
They've got Shubenacadie, Stewiacke too,
There's Pugwash and Sambro to name just a few.
Their Kejimkujik I count as fair ball,
Though it runs off the map to the neighbouring wall;

"Now Pubnico may be permitted to pass
And West Newdy Quoddy and Shinimicas.
Forgive Ecum Secum, let Washabuck stay,
Say nothing of Scatarie, Shepody Bay.
Pass over such fanciful names as Chegoggin's
But Gad! It's too much, sir, to call a place Joggins!"

Said Rand to McNally, "My name isn't Rand
If I'll permit such a weird place-name to stand.
Get out the eraser, pray hand me the shears.
It won't be my fault if such nonsense appears
(While vigour and health still permit me to rally)
On road map or atlas of Rand and McNally."

And snipping the letters clean out of the map,
He carefully rubbed the name right off the scrap
Till nothing remained but a vestige or less
Of Joggins, from 'J' to the ultimate 's'.
"Let there be no Joggins," said he, "on the hands
Of the noble McNallys or God-fearing Rands."

The pair in their rectitude sat for awhile
Each wearing a rather self-satisfied smile
And neither the mood nor the silence they broke
Until, with a start, 'twas McNally who spoke:
"There yet looms a problem we failed to foresee;
Pray what, if not Joggins, can such a place be?"

They picked up their pencils and sharpened their leads,
Adjusted their spectacles, scratched at their heads,
They scribbled and doodled and scrawled and erased,
They twiddled and fiddled and postured and paced;
They filled up their foolscap and addled their noggins
But neither could find a name better than Joggins.

They flirted with Flumbus and Willimaloo
And wondered if Dipstick or Drumble would do;
They thought about Thugmore, discarded Flagog,
Tried Scrumwater, Skoogle and Flapton-on-Frog,
Hacklerack, Humbug and Gosh-All-Toboggans
Without finding anything better than Joggins.

'Midst crumpled-up paper they pondered. And then,
"We're licked, Mr. R," muttered Mr. McN.
"We have to admit we should never have tried
Improving on Joggins, so let the thing ride.
'Twas Joggins we found it, and Joggins 'twill stay."
And Joggins, my friends, it remains to this day.

Halifax Harbour

Halifax Harbour, despite all we can do to change all that, remains one of the most attractive in the world, both commercially and esthetically. Still, it's time we stopped a practice that began in 1749 with the founding expedition under Edward Cornwallis.

On Halifax Harbour, the Queen of all Ports
The wavelets are dancing today
While various vessels of manifold sorts
Are plying the spume and the spray:
The high-stacked containers of overseas trade
Ride grandly past sloop, ketch and yawl
Whose spinnakers form a confetti parade.
The nautical charm of it all!
The tugboat, the tanker, the outboard, the skiff
Leave networks of foamy white wakes;
The wind from the westward is steady and stiff,
Ah! what a fine prospect it makes.
But what is this scum that discolours the froth,
These lumps on the waters that ride?
And what are those gouts of detestable broth
That rise from the depths of the tide?
What poisonous gases arrive at the nose
From yonder encrusted old tank,
And what is that muck-laden matter which flows
From pipes poking out of the bank?
Friends, these are but pages from history's lore,
Traditions that go with the town:
When colonists came to this beautiful shore
And anchors went rattling down
They emptied their chamberpots over the side,
Then gave them a salt-water rinse.
It just seemed so handy to dump in the tide,
We've all done the same ever since!

Black Rum and Blueberry Pie

Words and music by Jim Bennet

Black Rum and Blueberry Pie

Verse
We're livin' in the Age of Space, as ev'rybody knows;
Most everyone is in the race as this here country grows.
But down among the lobster pots you'll find a funny crew;
Us Maritimers don't do things like other people do. We just
    like…

Chorus
Fishin', fightin', gettin' tight 'n starin' at the sky,
Chewin', spittin' an' just sittin' watchin' things go by,
Climbin' rocks 'n drivin' oxen, learnin' how to lie,
Drinkin' black rum and eatin' blueberry pie.

Verse
I guess they worry 'bout us in them cities up the line.
They never will believe us when we say we're doin' fine;
They tell us we'd be better off if their rules was applied.
But why should they complain about the things they've
    never tried? Them things like…

Chorus

Verse
Now once upon a time some economic fellers came;
Development of human-type resources was their game.
They asked a big computer what us folks was fit to do;
It typed a great long list of things that we're best suited to.
    That list read…

Chorus

The Brain Drain

Our great-grandparents originated the proposition that Nova Scotia's greatest export is brains. From Thomas Chandler Haliburton of Windsor, creator of Sam Slick, who ended up in England, to Shelburne's Donald MacKay, the famous clipper ship designer who relocated in New York, we seem to have taken it on ourselves to replenish shortages of grey matter wherever they may exist. But let's remember that somebody has to stay on as breeding stock!

There's a great cerebral sewer called the Brain Drain
Where we pipe our Nova Scotian minds away.
We keep flushing mental giants down the Brain Drain,
And so few of us deep thinkers get to stay.
We've been sending all our talent to Toronto,
To Calgary, Vancouver and the States,
And it nearly makes me weep that for every one we keep,
There's twenty-seven more that relocates.

We send number-crunchin' wizards up to Bay Street,
And out there where the old Bow River flows;
Along that intellectual one-way street,
Our brightest and our best, they always goes!
There ain't no way to hang on to the smart ones
Exceptin' for a very, very few.
I guess I'm one of those, and so are you, I s'pose;
But without us what would Nova Scotia do?

If you scratch a big-time banker on the West Coast,
You'll likely find a Bluenose underneath
Who could've stayed put right here on the best coast
Drinkin' beer by Alexander Keith.
There's doctors and there's lawyers headin' westward,
And teachers and professors by the score
But I ain't gonna scurry down that road in any hurry,
'Cause someone's gotta stay and mind the store.

Now I know there's nothin' wrong with bein' famous
And I can't see any harm in gettin' rich;
But I'm gonna do it here or do it nowhere—
I ain't a-gonna be no runaway son-of-a-Nova Scotian.
So don't go lookin' for me up in Toronto,
'Cause I'm one guy you ain't a-gonna find.
And I jes' wanna let you know, if you ever do see me go
I'll be leavin' my brains behind!

Home Thoughts from Hogtown

Toronto's a fine, safe, hospitable city and all that—no longer the strait-laced, po-faced Dullsville we all used to hate. But still, there are times when a Nova Scotian's enjoyment of even the most alluring cities in the world can be overpowered by a flood tide of nostalgia.

The trees are full of apples in the Valley,
The beach is full of clams at Digby Neck,
The lobster's full of coral and tomalley,
The streets are full of tourists at Baddeck,
The boats are full of herring on the Fundy,
The Fundy's full of rusty-coloured mud,
The Solomon container's full of Gundy,
The forty-ouncer's full of Nelson's blood,
My head is full of thoughts of Nova Scotia,
My eyes are full of tears as they can be,
Toronto's full of over-priced hotel rooms
And one of them, alas, is full of me.

An Itch to Remember

Combinations, they were called: a type of winter underwear that incorporated leg, arm and torso parts along with the 'conveniences' of a fly front and a trap door at the rear. But when the coal furnace had guttered out overnight, many a schoolboy discovered that he'd lost the combination to the things. It was easier to don them standing on the cold floor; warmer (but definitely more complicated) to do so while still under the blankets. One family of torturers manufactured the brand worn by virtually all Nova Scotians. Maybe they keep a pair in the corporate museum as a multi-membered memento of the foundation of the family fortune.

Stanfields made them, and made them to last,
In Truro, the home of the good.
Those long-handled woolies of winters long past,
How great were the trials they withstood!
We've heard of old codgers who donned them each fall
And wore them all night and all day
Then shed what was left (which was not much at all)
The first decent weekend in May.
That wasn't the way with the urchins in town;
Our Stanfields each evening we'd doff.
We'd strain and we'd struggle, before bedding down,
To wrestle the wretched things off.
And there on the floor they would lie in a heap,
A terrible tangle of limbs
Which twisted and snarled as we lay there asleep,
With wooly, malevolent whims
Until, in the chill of the winter dawn's light,
We'd send forth a tentative hand
And grope for the snarl that had grown in the night
Whose twists we might not understand.
Then came the decision we faced every day,
The schoolboy's dilemma and curse:
To put the things on there was one awful way
And one that was possibly worse.
To stay beneath blankets meant warmth without fail;
To stand on the floor turned you blue.
But choosing the former meant dressing by Braille,

And that wasn't easy to do.
Yet he who emerged from the counterpane's hug
Exposing his gooseflesh all bare
Might find he was quicker, but vastly less snug;
The choice was both cruel and unfair.
For either way—dressing in warmth or in haste—
The process was sure to involve
Compounding those knots north and south of the waist
In ways no Houdini could solve.
Your arm down the leg and your head through the hatch,
A foot through the fly or the neck:
Appendage with aperture never would match
And the ordeal would leave you a wreck.
But once they were on, outside out, inside in,
Divested of splice, bend and hitch,
The torture began on your tender young skin;
Great God, how those woolies would itch!
And, given a blizzard while walking to school,
A roll in a snowbank as well,
A classroom whose heat grew increasingly cruel,
They gave off a smothering smell.
They'd bag and they'd sag and they'd stretch and they'd
    pull,
They'd droop at the knees and the nape:
A ludicrous, camel-like sculpture of wool
Ill-suited to human-like shape.
And then, at day's end, his adventures behind,
A lad would once more climb the stairs,
Crawl out of his longjohns and pay little mind,
Just let the things drop unawares
To lie inside out, interwoven and tied
In one sorry clump on the floor
Until the young fellow asleep at their side
Arose to confront them once more.

The Tingle of the Dingle

The Oxford English Dictionary will tell you that a dingle is a dell, usually shaded with trees. But to those familiar with the shores of the North West Arm on the west side of peninsular Halifax, it's not a generic, it's 'The Dingle,' a leafy bower with a tiny beach and a ferry wharf. The location has been dignified with the name Sir Sandford Fleming Park in honour of the famous railroad builder who donated it to the city. There's a tall Memorial Tower on a knoll above the beach, built to commemorate Responsible Government in Nova Scotia. But it's the Dingle and the Dingle Tower to everybody who comes to pick a berry or two, scan some light summer reading and dip an obligatory toe in the chilly salt water. As the years creep on, the dipping seems less obligatory.

At the Dingle we would mingle 'neath the shadow of the
 Tower,
There to wander and to ponder in the berry-laden bower
And to make our toe-tips tingle in the Dingle waters chill
To the cheerful obligato of the ripple of the rill.

We'd sing a pretty ditty to a ukulele tune:
Some jingle of the Dingle in the languid afternoon,
Or ease the weary grumble, near the tumble of the brook
With a poem from the pages of a well-remembered book.

But the digital diversion, the immersion in the brine
Of the pendulous extremities was wonderful and fine;
Not the book, the ukulele nor the berries, heaven knows,
Could match the Dingle-tingle of the titillated toes.

Old and married, young and single at the Dingle mingle
 still,
Toes to dangle 'neath the tangle of the birches on the hill
Where the shingle of the Dingle meets the tantalizing tide
And the shiny riffles ruffle where the periwinkles hide.

But the customary tingle of that Dingle-dipping toe
Is something now that jangles more than younger people
    know.
So I ramble through the bramble, pick my berries and
    depart,
Too old of toe for dipping, and, perhaps, at last too smart!

The Rewards of Writing Light

There can be a good deal of satisfaction in writing doggerel verse.
Money is a different matter. Oh, well! Those of us who do it can
still laugh all the way past the bank.

Light verse writers (silly blighters)
Strive for rhyme that's funny;
But since you ask, it's not the task
That's light, it's just the money.

Mordecai, that Richler guy,
Writes with lots of polish.
He'd starve (or worse) on silly verse
With subjects Montreal-ish.

Farley Mowat, don't you know it,
Writes what's far less risky:
Wolves and whales, not doggerel sales,
Buy cut plug and whiskey.

Richard Rohmer hits a homer
With each right-wing hero.
If his pen wrote whimsies, then
He'd be batting zero.

Margaret Atwood (never fat) would
End up even thinner
Were the dimes from comic rhymes
Her only source of dinner.

Comic verse and fat, full purse
Are mutually exclusive.
Laughs we may evoke, but pay,
Alas! is more elusive.

Pay no heed, ye doggerel breed;
Scrawl your comic squiggles.
Write, ye hacks; for there's no tax
On one who's paid in giggles.